THE COLOURFUL ME COLLECTION

Journey Three

Written by Simone Greaves
Illustrated by Anusha Hamza

First print January 2022

For Nylah, Naomi, Preston and Finlay,
with love always
x

4

When I wake on a winter's morning,
the sun is still sleeping at 6.
If I look carefully, I can see squirrels running around
collecting acorns while birds collect worms and sticks.

When I wake on a summer's morning,
the sun shines bright at 5.
The birds sing their sweet songs
to let us know the day has arrived.

For breakfast, I love to eat all kinds of cereal;
Kellogg's Rice Krispies, Cornflakes and Weetabix,
with cold milk in the summertime,
and hot milk for a warm winter fix.

Crumpets and bacon muffins go down a treat,
and a fry-up starts the day right
and makes my tummy feel full and complete.

Marmite on toast is not enjoyed by all,
but Daddy tells me that it will help me
grow strong and tall.

Mummy always encourages me to eat my fruit,
saying, "It will help your brain grow,"
something I never dispute.

Seasonal fruit help with our fruit bowl's colourful display.
Strawberries, raspberries and cherries don't last long or stay.

The warm months bring new tastes to enjoy and savour.
Apples and pears are included
in our traditional fruit flavours.

In the school playground, we play 'it',
what's the time Mr Wolf,
hide and seek, and hopscotch.

Sometimes we compete in races,
timed by teachers with stopwatches.

My country loves to compete in sport;
some are played in a field stadium or on a court.

Tennis games are swift,
cricket matches are long,
football will never become dated,
and rugby is full on.

All players work their hardest
to achieve medals of gold.
What fun it is to wave our country's flag
in the summer's heat or winters cold.

White and red, the colours are bold and bright;
can you guess my country
with these flag colours in sight?

Cricket is our national game,
which great players over many years
have helped our sport to reach its fame.

I protect my wickets with my bat,
I prepare for spin bowling and swap
my helmet for my hat.

We get our runs in one, two and threes,
before the fielders return the ball quickly.
I always aim to hit a 6,
the ball clears the boundaries
without bouncing or, even better,
a spectator catches it.

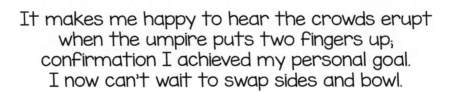

It makes me happy to hear the crowds erupt
when the umpire puts two fingers up;
confirmation I achieved my personal goal.
I now can't wait to swap sides and bowl.

50
02
10

Our capital city has history
that dates back to the Roman times.
One of the most famous landmarks
that towers overhead is Big Ben.
I love to hear when his five bells chime.

There's an eye that steadily moves around,
watching all without making a sound,
and a building in the shape of a gherkin
reaches high from the ground.

Magnificent crown jewels
are closely guarded in a royal palace fortress,
and a drawbridge built in 1886 grants
tall ships continued river access.

Gone are the days of horses and carts,
boats that congested the river Thames
while they arrive and depart.

Our famous river was once always busy for business,
but now its boats sail mainly for leisure purposes.

Markets, shops and museums
filled with historical wonders line our streets.
Busy roads with black cabs
and red double decker buses zoom past,
and not all passengers have a seat.

The roads are above and the tube lines are below,
connecting each station
with passengers that travel to and fro.

Buildings dominate, parks are scarcely seen,
restaurants and cafes
are open to all tastes of cuisine.

When the day turns to night everything comes alight,
the magical city that never sleeps continues to shine bright.

This is a picture of three different countries in one.

Can you guess which is mine
and touch it with your thumb?

Mini beast hunts are a favourite adventure all year round.
Snails, worms and woodlouse can all be found
under logs and in the muddy ground.

In the spring and summertime,
bumblebees, butterflies,
little lady birds and dragonflies
join the birds flying high,
while squirrels and rabbits hop
and jump trying to reach the sky.

Deer are wild in the parks and foxes prowl at night,
and owls have super night vision
searching for a midnight snack under the moonlight.

On the farm, cows give milk,
sheep share wool,
chickens lay their eggs,
and horses help the farmer work the land
with their very strong legs.

Pigs play in the mud and roosters crow,
wishing everyone good morning.

Sometimes this can make us jump
as it's usually without warning.

The playpark is the after school hot spot
where we skip, hop and run.
When it's the summertime,
we have outdoor playdates
and yummy picnics to make the most
of the warm summer sun.

We like to go on the swings
to see how high we can fly.
I like to see if my toes
can touch the sky.

We hide in the tunnels
and slide down the slides.
Big or small,
everyone gets a ride.

When the sun is hot,
the water comes to spray,
cooling us down
after a long and hot summers day.

The summer holidays are fun
filled with many ways to pass time.
Through the long grass we run,
and up to the top of the trees we climb.

We take our nets to the streams
and paddle our toes,
and in the fields we pick buttercups
to see if our chins glow.

We lay back in the grass
to spot wonderful shapes in the clouds.
In the parks we are close to the wonders of nature,
far away from the city crowds.

Here the breeze blows, and the crickets sing.
We make daisy chains
and transform into princesses and kings.

Foraging is one of my favourite things to do,
reaching high to pick crunchy apples,
cherries and plums, too.

With different shades of summer berries,
I can't help but eat a few.

My mum says, she would love
to have the queen over for afternoon tea.
"Put the kettle on love,"
is her favourite favour to ask of me.

In our capital city, a royal palace can be found,
the Queen's castle home, however,
is found on the other side of town.

The Queen spends her weekends
surrounded by lush royal grounds of green
with an avenue of beautiful chestnut and plane trees.

The Queen is very lucky
as she has a choice of which home to roam,
throwing royal banquets and tea parties
with a unique royal tone.

Our weather is temperate,
ranging from cold to warm often rainy and mild.
The summertime brings BBQs,
paddling pools and beach trips to the seaside.

Here, we enjoy splashing in the cold sea,
watching the ships sail
while eating fish and chips
this is what makes me happy.

We visit the old sweet shops,
where sweeties of all different shapes and sizes
fill the beautiful brightly coloured rainbow jars,
gleaming like wonderful prizes.

While at the seaside,
my first choice is always a stick of rock,
and my grandad always chooses popping candy
because he likes to hear them pop!

If we are lucky,
the winter will bring us beautiful white snow.
I love to catch a glimpse of a red robin breast
when he flies by to say hello!

Autumn leaves dance in the wind,
off the tree they must go.
Spring and summer seem far away now,
but the essence of magic, we know,
will continue to surprise us
as the seasons come and go.

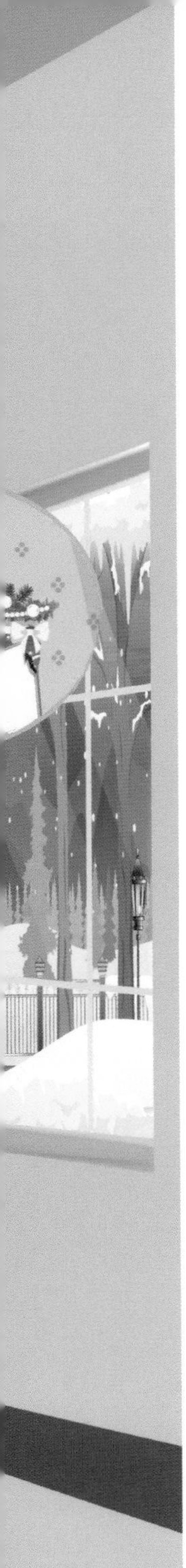

In the summertime
when I lay in my bed at night
I sometimes struggle to sleep
as the sun is still hot and bright.

The winter sun sets by 4pm,
and I love days like these when,
with foggy windows and icy cold toes.
The heating is turned up
and the windows are tightly closed.

It's times like these that
I enjoy a cosy winter night
with hot chocolate
warming our tummies
and Christmas in sight.

I'm colourful me, I'm colourful me.

From my country you can see
everything that makes me, me:

not my skin colour or my hair,
for it's what's on the inside of my body
that makes me, me.

I think by now, you might have guessed...

I am English!

My country is England!

For your next adventure, where would you like to visit?

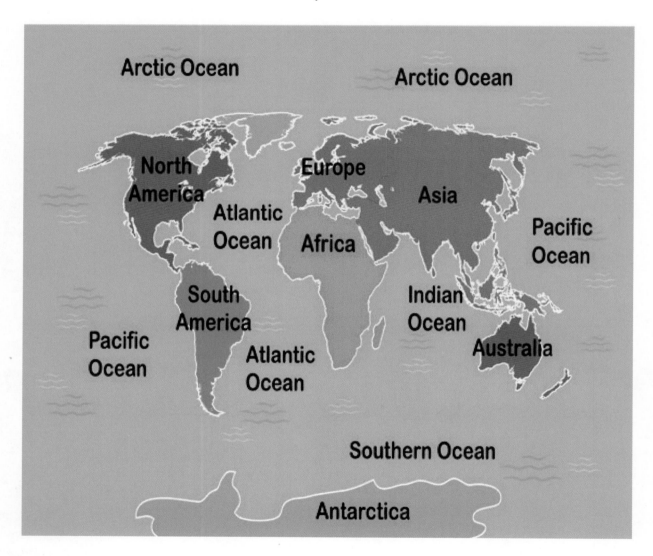

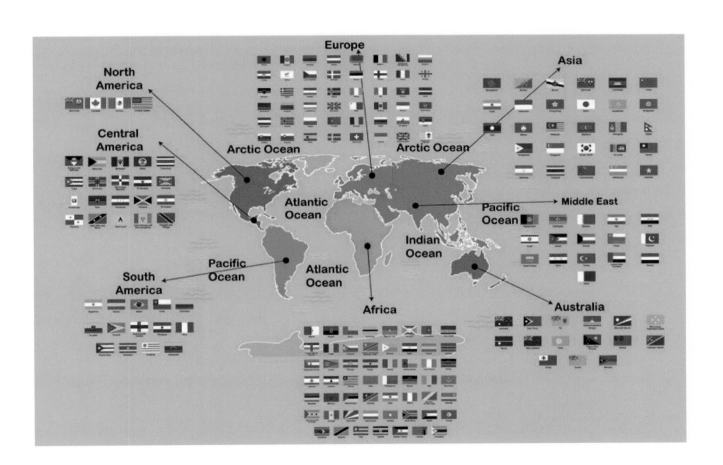

Capital cities in Europe

Country	Capital City	Country	Capital City
Åland Islands	Mariehamn	Latvia	Riga
Albania	Tirana	Liechtenstein	Vaduz
Andorra	Andorra la Vella	Lithuania	Vilnius
Austria	Vienna	Luxembourg	Luxembourg
Belarus	Minsk	Malta	Valletta
Belgium	Brussels	Moldova	Chişinău
Bosnia and Herzegovina	Sarajevo	Monaco	Monaco
Bulgaria	Sofia	Montenegro	Podgorica
Croatia	Zagreb	Netherlands	Amsterdam
Czechia	Prague	North Macedonia	Skopje
Denmark	Copenhagen	Norway	Oslo
Estonia	Tallinn	Poland	Warsaw
Faroe Islands	Tórshavn	Portugal	Lisbon
Finland	Helsinki	Romania	Bucharest
France	Paris	Russia	Moscow
Germany	Berlin	San Marino	San Marino
Gibraltar	Gibraltar	Serbia	Belgrade
Greece	Athens	Slovakia	Bratislava
Guernsey	Saint Peter Port	Slovenia	Ljubljana
Hungary	Budapest	Spain	Madrid
Iceland	Reykjavík	Svalbard	Longyearbyen
Ireland	Dublin	Sweden	Stockholm
Isle of Man	Douglas	Switzerland	Bern
Italy	Rome	Ukraine	Kiev
Jersey	Saint Helier	United Kingdom	London
Kosovo	Pristina		

Capital cities in the Americas

Country	Capital City	Country	Capital City
Anguilla	The Valley	Guyana	Georgetown
Antigua and Barbuda	Saint John's	Haiti	Port-au-Prince
Argentina	Buenos Aires	Honduras	Tegucigalpa
Aruba	Oranjestad	Jamaica	Kingston
Bahamas	Nassau	Martinique	Fort-de-France
Barbados	Bridgetown	Mexico	Mexico City
Belize	Belmopan	Montserrat	Plymouth
Bermuda	Hamilton	Nicaragua	Managua
Bolivia	Sucre	Panama	Panama City
Brazil	Brasília	Paraguay	Asunción
British Virgin Islands	Road Town	Peru	Lima
Canada	Ottawa	Puerto Rico	San Juan
Cayman Islands	George Town	Saint Barthelemy	Gustavia
Chile	Santiago	Saint Kitts and Nevis	Basseterre
Colombia	Bogotá	Saint Lucia	Castries
Costa Rica	San José	Saint Martin	Marigot
Cuba	Havana	Saint Pierre and Miquelon	Saint-Pierre
Curacao	Willemstad	Saint Vincent and the Grenadines	Kingstown
Dominca	Roseau	Sint Maarten	Philipsburg
Dominican Republic	Santo Domingo	South Georgia and South Sandwich Islands	King Edward Point
Ecuador	Quito	Suriname	Paramaribo
El Salvador	San Salvador	Trinidad and Tobago	Port of Spain
Falkland Islands	Stanley	Turks and Caicos Islands	Cockburn Town
French Guiana	Cayenne	United States	Washington, D.C.
Greenland	Nuuk	Uruguay	Montevideo
Grenada	Saint George's	Venezuela	Caracas
Guadeloupe	Basse-Terre	Virgin Islands	Charlotte Amalie
Guatemala	Guatemala City		

Capital cities in Asia

Country	Capital City	Country	Capital City
Afghanistan	Kabul	Macau	Concelho de Macau
Armenia	Yerevan	Malaysia	Kuala Lumpur
Azerbaijan	Baku	Maldives	Malé
Bahrain	Manama	Mongolia	Ulaanbaatar
Bangladesh	Dhaka	Nepal	Kathmandu
Bhutan	Thimphu	North Korea	Pyongyang
Brunei	Bandar Seri Begawan	Oman	Muscat
Burma	Nay Pyi Taw	Pakistan	Islamabad
Cambodia	Phnom Penh	Palestine	Ramallah
China	Beijing	Philippines	Manila
Cyprus	Nicosia	Qatar	Doha
East Timor	Dili	Saudi Arabia	Riyadh
Georgia	Tbilisi	Singapore	Singapore
Hong Kong	Hong Kong	South Korea	Seoul
India	New Delhi	Sri Lanka	Colombo
Indonesia	Jakarta	Syria	Damascus
Iran	Tehran	Taiwan	Taipei
Iraq	Baghdad	Tajikistan	Dushanbe
Israel	Jerusalem	Thailand	Bangkok
Japan	Tokyo	Turkey	Ankara
Jordan	Amman	Turkmenistan	Ashgabat
Kazakhstan	Nur-Sultan	United Arab Emirates	Abu Dhabi
Kuwait	Kuwait City	Uzbekistan	Tashkent
Kyrgyzstan	Bishkek	Vietnam	Hanoi
Laos	Vientiane	Yemen	Sanaa
Lebanon	Beirut		

Capital cities on the Australian continent

Country	Capital City
Australia	Canberra
Christmas Island	Flying Fish Cove
Cocos (Keeling) Islands	West Island
New Zealand	Wellington
Norfolk Island	Kingston

Capital cities in Africa

Country	Capital City	Country	Capital City
Algeria	Algiers	Sierra Leone	Freetown
Angola	Luanda	Gambia	Banjul
Benin	Porto-Novo	Ghana	Accra
Botswana	Gaborone	Guinea	Conakry
Burkina Faso	Ouagadougou	Guinea-Bissau	Bissau
Burundi	Bujumbura	Ivory Coast	Yamoussoukro
Cameroon	Yaoundé	Kenya	Nairobi
Cape Verde	Praia	Lesotho	Maseru
Central African Republic	Bangui	Liberia	Monrovia
Chad	N'Djamena	Libya	Tripoli
Comoros	Moroni	Madagascar	Antananarivo
Democratic Republic of the Congo	Kinshasa	Malawi	Lilongwe
Djibouti	Djibouti	Mali	Bamako
Egypt	Cairo	Mauritania	Nouakchott
Eqatorial Guinea	Malabo	Mauritius	Port Louis
Eritrea	Asmara	Mayotte	Mamoudzou
Eswatini	Mbabane	Morocco	Rabat
Ethiopia	Addis Ababa	Mozambique	Maputo
Gabon	Libreville	Somalia	Mogadishu
Namibia	Windhoek	South Africa	Pretoria
Niger	Niamey	South Sudan	Juba
Nigeria	Abuja	Sudan	Khartoum
Republic of the Congo	Brazzaville	Tanzania	Dodoma
Reunion	Saint-Denis	Togo	Lomé
Rwanda	Kigali	Tunisia	Tunis
Saint Helena and Tristan da Cunha	Jamestown	Uganda	Kampala
Sao Tome and Principe	São Tomé	Western Sahara	El Aaiún
Senegal	Dakar	Zambia	Lusaka
Seychelles	Victoria	Zimbabwe	Harare

Capital cities of Oceania

Country	Capital City
American Samoa	Pago Pago
Cook Islands	Avarua
Fiji	Suva
French Polynesia	Papeete
Guam	Hagåtña
Kiribati	Tarawa
Marshall Islands	Majuro
Nauru	Yaren
New Caledonia	Nouméa
Niue	Alofi
Northern Mariana Islands	Saipan
Papua New Guinea	Port Moresby
Pitcairn Islands	Adamstown
Samoa	Apia
Solomon Islands	Honiara
Tonga	Nuku'alofa
Tuvalu	Funafuti
Vanuatu	Port Vila
Wallis and Futuna	Matā'utu

Famous world landmarks and their descriptions

Big Ben

Big Ben is the nickname for the Great Bell of the striking clock at the north end of the Palace of Westminster; the name is frequently extended to also refer to the clock and the clock tower in England's capital city London.

Christ the Redeemer

Located in Brazil at the 700-metre peak of Corcovado mountain in the Tijuca Forest National Park, Christ the Redeemer overlooks the city of Rio de Janeiro. He is a symbol of Christianity across the world and has become a cultural icon of both Rio de Janeiro and Brazil. Christ the Redeemer was also voted one of the New Seven Wonders of the World.

The Taj Mahal

Found in New Delhi, The Taj Mahal sits on the southern bank of the river Yamuna in the Indian city of Agra. The tomb is the centrepiece of a 17-hectare (42-acre) complex. This complex includes a mosque and a guest house which are set in formal gardens bound on three sides by a defence wall.

Mount Kenya

Mount Kenya is the highest mountain in Kenya and the second highest in Africa, after Kilimanjaro. The highest peaks of the mountain are Batian, Nelion and Point Lenana.

The Great Wall of China

The Great Wall of China is a series of fortifications that were built across the historical northern borders of ancient Chinese states and Imperial China as protection against various nomadic groups from the Eurasian Steppe.

Niagara Falls

Niagara Falls is a group of three waterfalls at the southern end of Niagara Gorge. These amazing fall's stretch from the borders of the province of Ontario in Canada and the state of New York in the United States.

Parliament Buildings, Barbados

The Parliament Buildings, found in Bridgetown, are the seat of the Parliament of Barbados. Built between 1870 and 1874, the buildings have been the meeting place for both chambers of Parliament since 16 June 1874.

Sydney Opera house

The Sydney Opera House is a multi-venue performing arts centre on Sydney Harbour in Australia. It is one of the 20th century's most famous and distinctive buildings.

For updates on the latest Colourful me journey releases,
please visit us on our Instagram page:

 /the_colourful_me_collection

Here you will be able to find information on where you can visit next!

Printed in Great Britain
by Amazon